# The Split History of the

# NORMAN CONQUEST

## THE NORMAN PERSPECTIVE

BY NICK HUNTER

CONTENT CONSULTANT:
Dr Linsey Hunter
Lecturer and Teaching Assistant at the University of the

Raintree is an imprint of Capstone Global Library Limited, a company incorporated in England and Wales having its registered office at 264 Banbury Road, Oxford, OX2 7DY – Registered company number: 6695582

www.raintree.co.uk
myorders@raintree.co.uk

Edited by Helen Cox Cannons
Designed by Philippa Jenkins
Original illustrations © Capstone Global Library Ltd 2016
Picture research by Kelly Garvin
Production by Victoria Fitzgerald
Originated by Capstone Global Library Ltd
Printed and bound in China

ISBN 978 1 4747 2669 6
20 19 18 17 16
10 9 8 7 6 5 4 3 2 1

## ACKNOWLEDGEMENTS

We would like to thank the following for permission to reproduce photographs:
**Norman Perspective:** Bridgeman Images/Manners of the Normans, Coronation of William the Conqueror, English School, (19th Century)/Private Collection/Look and Learn, 24; Getty Images/ Print Collector, 27; Mary Evans Picture Library, cover (bottom), Edwin Mullen Collection, cover (top); Newscom: akg-images/British Library, 21, akg-images/Werner Forman, 5 (t), Alisdair Macdonald/REX, 29, CMSP Education, 7, Karl F. Schofmann imageBROKER, 11, Walter Rawlings/Robert Harding, 13, World History Archive, 9, 15; North Wind Picture Archives, 17, 19; Oxford Designers and Illustrators, 5 (b); Shutterstock/Lance Bellers, 23.
**Anglo-Saxon Perspective:** Alamy/Mary Evans Picture Library, 17; Art Resource/The Trustees of the British Museum, 5; Getty Images: Culture Club, 29, Hulton Archive, 21, Popperfoto, 10, Print Collector, 27, Universal History Archive/UIG, 24; Mary Evans Picture Library, cover (top), 23, Edwin Mullen Collection, cover (bottom); Newscom: akg-photos/Bristish Library, 14, UPPA/ Photoshot, 7, World History Archive, 13; Oxford Designers and Illustrators, 19; Shutterstock/ godrick, 9.

Every effort has been made to contact copyright holders of material reproduced in this book. Any omissions will be rectified in subsequent printings if notice is given to the publisher.

All the internet addresses (URLs) given in this book were valid at the time of going to press. However, due to the dynamic nature of the internet, some addresses may have changed, or sites may have changed or ceased to exist since publication. While the author and publisher regret any inconvenience this may cause readers, no responsibility for any such changes can be accepted by either the author or the publisher.

# Contents

## SHARED RESOURCES

# CHAPTER 1

# THE RISE OF THE NORMANS

The year 1066 is one of the most important dates in English history. That year, William, Duke of Normandy won a great victory over Harold Godwinson to claim the English crown. But this Norman invasion had its roots many years before 1066.

During the 10th century AD, Vikings from what are now Norway, Sweden and Denmark sailed south to raid the coasts of Europe. They also settled in new lands, including the north-east of England and northern France. By the 11th century, this area in France was called Normandy. Its people were Christian and their leaders spoke French and took French names, but the Normans were fiercely independent of the French king.

England's people had lived through years of battles and plots to steal the crown. Viking King Cnut had seized the British crown in 1016. Cnut had murdered most of the family of the previous king, Aethelred, so that no one could challenge his power. The earls of England, including the most powerful of all, Earl Godwine, supported Cnut, mainly because Cnut had also murdered many earls

# NORMAN PRINCES

Aethelred's wife was Norman and two of his sons, Princes Edward and Alfred, fled to Normandy. They spent over 25 years there, waiting for the death of Cnut and his sons. They grew up as brothers to William's father, Duke Robert of Normandy. They begged the Duke of Normandy to protect them from murderous King Cnut. In 1033, Robert planned to invade England to drive Cnut from the throne and make Edward king, but bad weather put an end to this plan.

*This is part of a longship, which the Vikings used to attack the coasts of Northern Europe. The Vikings, or Norsemen, gave Normandy its name.*

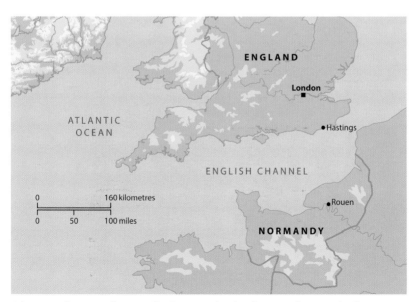

*The coast of Normandy was a day's voyage by ship from southern England.*

Edward returned to England in 1042 as king, after the death of Cnut and his sons. Edward chose his Norman friends to help him govern. He also chose a Norman to be Archbishop of Canterbury, the most powerful job in the English Church. The deeply religious king earned the name Edward the Confessor.

King Edward was, by then, an old man and found it hard to deal with the powerful nobles' demands. The council of English earls, named the Witenagemot, including Earl Godwine, had supported Edward's enemies. As Edward had no children, the earls thought they would choose the next king.

While Edward tried to survive in England, a new force was making waves in Normandy. His name was William, Duke of Normandy. William was eight when his father, Duke Robert, died. William faced many enemies of his own and, during his childhood, he even witnessed the murder of his servant. But the young duke was tough and determined to succeed. As William reached adulthood, he defeated a rebellion at the Battle of Val-ès-Dunes in 1047. Although he still had to deal with some resistance, this victory helped William establish himself as Normandy's leader.

King Edward was much older than William but he would have known William as a child. Edward's problems with Godwine made him friendlier towards the Normans who had helped him as a young man.

# WILLIAM THE CONQUEROR

William was not called "the Conqueror" until
after his death, but he was already respected
and feared as a young man. By the standards
of his time, William was a huge man, renowned
for his strength. The Bayeux Tapestry shows
William with no beard and his hair cut short at
the back. William dealt with many attempts to
overthrow him. This taught him to deal brutally
with rebels. During a siege of a town in southern
Normandy, soldiers from a neighbouring region
mocked William from the safety of a castle. When
the duke captured it, he ordered that the men
should be maimed as a warning to others.

*William, Duke of Normandy*

# EDWARD'S HEIR

According to later Norman writers, Edward the Confessor sent a message to William in 1051. The letter promised that William would be King of England after Edward's death. Later that year, after Edward had sent Godwine into exile, William visited Edward in England. The two leaders sealed an alliance.

William had plenty of enemies to keep him busy, including Henry I, King of France. Edward's enemies were not quite beaten either. Godwine returned to his position as England's leading noble. When he died in 1053, his son Harold Godwinson took on his father's role as England's most powerful man and the unwilling King Edward's right-hand man.

In 1064, William finally got to meet Harold. According to the Normans, Harold was sent to Normandy to confirm Edward's plan to hand William the crown. English sources, however, claim that Harold was shipwrecked and the Normans captured him. During this visit, Harold swore an oath to William in the presence of holy relics. This made it a sacred promise.

The Normans argued that in swearing this oath Harold had promised to serve William and to help him become King of England. They thought that Harold would not dare to break the promise, especially one made to a fearsome warrior like William. When Edward died in January 1065, William prepared to accept the crown of England.

# THE BAYEUX TAPESTRY

One of the reasons we know so much about the Normans and their invasion of England is the Bayeux Tapestry. This huge piece of embroidery is nearly 70 metres (230 feet) long. It shows the main events of the Norman Conquest from William's meeting with Harold Godwinson in 1064. The Tapestry was probably made on the orders of Bishop Odo of Bayeux, William's half-brother, so it tells the Norman version of the story. It has been claimed that it was stitched in Canterbury, England.

*In this section of the Bayeux Tapestry, Harold is shown swearing an oath to help William of Normandy.*

# A PROMISE BROKEN

Harold did not waste any time deciding whether to break the oath to William. The day after Edward the Confessor's death in January 1066, Harold had himself crowned King of England.

Duke William was out hunting when he learned that Harold was King of England. The fiery Norman was speechless with rage. According to one report "he spoke to no man, neither dared any man speak to him" . William returned immediately to his castle to plot his next move.

Harold had sworn to be loyal to William, and to help him become King of England. William's troubled childhood and the constant struggle to maintain his power taught him to value loyalty above everything else. Harold had spent time with William and he should have known that William would not accept Harold's betrayal without a fight.

William immediately sent an outraged message to Harold. The new King of England replied that the council of England's leading earls had chosen him and he could not refuse. This was true, but Harold had been crowned the day after Edward the Confessor's death – would he have

# PLOTTING REVENGE

William was angry, but he had to plan his next move calmly and carefully. If he wanted to be King of England, he would need the support of all the nobles and knights across Normandy. They had to obey him in Normandy but William could not force his followers to risk their lives in a foreign battle. He would also need to justify his actions to other kings and the Pope, the leader of the Roman Catholic Church.

William's plan was to convince the Pope that his invasion of England was much more than a squabble over who would be king. It was actually a holy war.

*William was always careful to keep in favour with the Church. He built great centres for worship and learning, such as Jumièges Abbey in Normandy.*

## THE POWER OF RELIGION

The Catholic Church was the most powerful authority in Medieval Europe, and the ultimate power in the Church lay with the Pope in Rome. Most Medieval people in Europe believed in the Christian God. They thought they had to obey the Church if they wanted to go to heaven when they died. The Church controlled vast lands and wealth. There were no printing presses in the 11th century and very few people could read or write, so all books and documents were written by hand, usually by monks. As a result, the authority of the Church was rarely questioned.

In 1052, the Godwines had sacked the Norman Archbishop of Canterbury and replaced him with the English Stigand. Choosing archbishops was the Pope's job. The Pope did not like it when kings started interfering, especially as Stigand had been excommunicated, or outlawed, from the Church. If William could invade England and remove this archbishop, he would be doing God's work. That was enough to convince the Pope to support him, and with Church support, nobles from Normandy and beyond rushed to fight alongside William.

William ordered his men to start building a great fleet of ships in the early months of 1066. These ships would carry thousands of soldiers and horses, along with the armour and weapons they would need to defeat the Anglo-Saxon warriors of England.

# A GOOD OMEN

In the final week of April 1066, the people of England and Normandy saw a bright light in the sky. One watcher described it as a "long-haired star". We now know that it was a comet that passes close to Earth every 76 years, called Halley's Comet. In England, this was seen as a bad sign from God. The Normans believed it signalled that a change was coming somewhere, and they thought they knew where.

*The Normans had no idea that the bright star they saw was a comet, now known as Halley's Comet.*

# CHAPTER 3

# PREPARING TO INVADE

William was an experienced soldier and he knew that an invasion of England was risky. Harold and his earls could call on the loyalty of thousands of professional and part-time soldiers. The English had more ships than the Normans. They would also be fighting on home ground. The south coast of England was Harold's own land and he would not give it up without a fight. If William failed, he was risking his own life and the lives of thousands of his followers.

William had to persuade his knights that victory was possible. Having the Pope's support helped, but William asked each of his nobles to pledge as many ships as they could to the invasion. William's closest advisers agreed to provide 60 ships each and his two half-brothers supplied more than 100. The fleet William put together at the mouth of the River Dives in Normandy included

## HORSE POWER

William's fleet did not just carry soldiers. The ships included space for around 6,000 horses. Each knight needed three horses: his warhorse for battle, and two smaller horses to carry weapons and the knight's squire, or servant.

Across the channel, Harold had stationed his army along the south coast, ready to react when an enemy sail was spotted. There was one important factor that neither side could control – the weather. William's square-sailed ships could not cross the English Channel against the wind. Once the fleet was ready in August 1066, there was nothing they could do but wait. While they waited, the army and their horses were supplied with huge amounts of food and drink.

*Not all of William's ships were built from scratch but those that were involved hundreds of men chopping down trees or stitching the sails of the wooden longboats.*

# HELP FROM THE NORTH

William and Harold were not the only rivals fighting for the crown.
Harold's brother Tostig had attempted his own attack from the sea in
the spring of 1066. It was unsuccessful but Tostig and his brother were
enemies, and he wasn't about to give up. He went looking for allies and
found Harald Hardrada, King of Norway. Together they planned an
invasion in the north of England.

The English army were tired of waiting for William's forces to
arrive. On 8 September 1066, Harold dismissed his soldiers so that
they could go and collect the annual harvest.

Once he heard the news that Harold's soldiers were allowed to
return home, William was desperate to get moving as soon as he could.
He took a chance and set sail towards England. But William's hasty
decision nearly ended in disaster. The ships were blown back to the
French coast and some were wrecked. The Normans would have to
try again.

Fortunately for William, Harold was forced to recall his army
and march north instead, to deal with the invading forces of Harald
Hardrada. The English won a great victory at the Battle of Stamford
Bridge on 25 September, but then they had to march south again in
order to reassemble and face the coming attack from Normandy.

Meanwhile, the wind had changed in the English Channel. The
Normans were ready to invade. When he set sail on 27 September,
William could not have heard about Harold's victory at Stamford
Bridge. He did not know if he'd be fighting the English or the Vikings.

# NORMAN KNIGHTS

William's army included hundreds of mounted
knights. They wore helmets and **hauberks** made of
metal scales or mail (see picture). This armour
weighed around 14 kilograms (31 pounds).
William's knights were armed with swords and
lances. They were not the "knights in shining
armour" that we think of today. War was a
brutal business and soldiers would often collect
replacement pieces of armour or weapons from
dead bodies on the battlefield.

*This is an artist's impression of Norman knights.*

# VICTORY AT HASTINGS

CHAPTER 4

On 27 September 1066, the Norman army set sail. William led the way on his ship *Mona*. They sailed through the night and when dawn broke, William discovered that his ship was all alone. The duke waited for the rest of his fleet to catch up. If any English ships had been patrolling that area, William could have been captured and the invasion would have been over before it had even started.

The Norman fleet headed for the small, southern port of Pevensey. As they sailed into the bay, they saw the walls of an ancient Roman fort. They could use the fort as a stronghold against English attacks. They also seized another fort along the coast at Hastings.

## BATTLE READY

Soon after landing, William heard about Harold's victory at Stamford Bridge. The English would have gained confidence from defeating such a dangerous enemy, but it was too late for William to turn back now. His best chance was to face Harold's army as soon as possible, before the English king could gather a larger force.

The thousands of Norman soldiers and horses needed food and other supplies. While waiting to sail, they had been careful not to steal supplies from the local Norman people. In England, nothing was off limits. William also wanted to send a message to Harold: Harold was the lord of southern England and he had a duty to protect his people. William's army burned villages and people were forced to flee. They had no one to protect them, unless Harold could get there quickly. That was exactly what William wanted.

William sent knights to watch for signs that Harold's army was approaching. Both sides knew that they might gain an advantage if they could surprise the other. Rather than waiting at his fortress in Hastings, at dawn on 14 October, William ordered his forces to march north to meet the English army.

*Pevensey was a perfect landing place for the Norman army.*

The two armies finally faced each other a few miles north of Hastings. The Normans were nervous as they looked at the English army on Senlac Ridge. William reminded his troops that they had never lost a battle. The English were used to losing, and this battle would be no different. The two armies were probably about the same size, but there were some big differences.

## THE NORMAN ARMY

In contrast with the English wall of shields, the Normans planned to defeat their enemy with three lines of attack. At the head of the Norman army were the archers, armed with crossbows. After trumpets had signalled the start of the battle, the archers fired a volley of arrows. The crossbow was the latest military technology. The arrows pierced shields and caused panic in the English lines before the two sides met in bloody hand-to-hand contact.

Behind the archers were the infantry, foot soldiers in heavy armour and wielding swords. These troops had to try and break the English shield wall. But in this bloody struggle using swords, axes and spears, the English were strongest.

Finally came the fast-moving cavalry of William, his nobles and knights riding warhorses. These were the stars of the Norman army. Once the shield wall was broken, their swift attacks would devastate the part-time soldiers to the rear of the English army. The Normans were amazed that the English did not ride their own horses into battle.

# A BLOODY STRUGGLE

The Normans found the English wall of shields very difficult to break. The English were happy to keep their defensive position and the Normans knew that if they could not break through, they would be lucky to escape from England with their lives. As their waves of attack failed, a rumour went round the confused battlefield that William was dead.

*This painting of the Battle of Hastings was made in Rouen, France, in the late 15th century.*

Some Normans began to retreat. Some reports of the battle claimed it was a deliberate tactic to break the English defences. As the Normans retreated, William removed his helmet to show that he was alive and urged his soldiers forward again. This was the turning point in the battle. The English line was starting to break. As exhaustion set in, the cavalry and archers gave the Normans a decisive advantage.

The Battle of Hastings was fought to decide who would be King of England. If William or Harold were to be killed, then the battle would effectively be over. Harold fought at the centre of his army, and late in the day he was killed. The Bayeux Tapestry shows Harold being shot in the eye with an arrow, but other sources claim that William sent hand-picked knights to target the English leader.

As news of Harold's death spread, the English army started to escape as best they could. The Normans' military skill and tactics had won the day, but William knew that the conquest of England was far from over.

## AFTER THE BATTLE

William had grown up knowing that he needed to be ruthless to keep his power in Normandy. There were still powerful English earls with armies of their own who might try to oppose him. He waited a few days to give them a chance to surrender. When this did not happen, William decided to show them what would happen if they fought against him. The Normans rampaged through southern England, burning villages and executing those who opposed them.

One by one, the earls and archbishops of England surrendered to the Normans. Sensibly, the remaining English troops had gathered in London. William decided it was too risky to cross London Bridge and attack the city. Instead he captured towns around London and encircled the city. By the time he reached the capital, his most powerful enemies had surrendered. William was ready to take the crown.

*The place where William defeated Harold was later called Battle. William built a great abbey there, named Battle Abbey, to thank God for his victory and to make up for the sin of killing a monarch.*

# CHAPTER 5
# CONQUERING THE ENGLISH

William, Duke of Normandy was crowned King William I in Westminster Abbey on 25 December 1066. That fateful year had seen three different kings of England and several bloody battles fought on English soil. William planned to bring peace and stability to England, but he and his followers were still wary of possible rebels.

*William was the second king to be crowned in Westminster Abbey that year.*

During the coronation, the shouts and cheers as the new king was crowned spooked Abbey guards. Fearing an uprising, they decided to set fire to the buildings around the Abbey as a distraction. This was not the best start for the new king and the people of London.

It did not take the shine off William's triumph. A few months later, he returned to Normandy to celebrate his victory with his own people. Taking no chances, he captured three English earls and took them with him as hostages. This was a warning to anyone wanting to cause trouble in England.

## CLASH OF CULTURES

Back in England, the Normans were making big changes and not everyone liked them. William's Norman supporters expected reward for risking their lives to help him defeat Harold. The king gave each of them some land in his new kingdom. Each was expected to build a castle and control the English in his part of the country.

William allowed his new English subjects to keep some of their land as long as they accepted his rule. But English anger at the new Norman overlords boiled over in 1069. William faced a wave of rebellions across the north of England. His troops at Durham were massacred and the rebels besieged York. His attempt to be fair had failed. Now William would have to act.

The English knew of William's reputation for ruthless revenge on anyone who challenged his authority. The people of northern England felt the force of his anger. Their towns and crops were destroyed. Those rebels who were not killed faced the threat of starvation.

After 1069, Norman England was much quieter. William was able to impose his own ideas, although he still faced plots and rebellions in both England and Normandy. Even if daily life did not change that much for the ordinary Anglo-Saxon people of England, things changed forever for those who had been wealthy and powerful before the invasion. William the Conqueror left England a very different country from the one he had invaded in 1066.

## CASTLES AND CATHEDRALS

The most obvious sign of Norman rule was their castles. The Anglo-Saxon kings had built walls and fortifications, but it was the Normans who brought castles to England. They built around 1,000 castles in the century after 1066. Castles allowed the nobles and knights to dominate the surrounding countryside, and these impressive buildings were a constant reminder of who was in charge. They were built to last a long time, and many Norman castles still stand today in England.

Religion was a vital part of Norman society; after all, the Pope himself had supported the Norman invasion of England. As well as castles, the Normans built stone churches and cathedrals up and down the country. Many of them, such as the great cathedral at Durham, are still impressive today. To the people of 11th-century England, these great stone buildings towering over the landscape were totally awe-inspiring.

*A typical Norman castle had a strong tower, or keep, built on a mound called a motte. The bailey was the walled enclosure around the keep.*

## NORMAN RULE

The Normans changed the way Britain was ruled. The council of leading earls, which had supported Harold as king, no longer existed under William. Instead, when a monarch died, his or her eldest son would become king, although things could get a bit more complicated if there was no eldest son. Lords could now pass on their lands to the next generation, but they were expected to serve the king, especially in times of war. The peasants who lived on the land served their lord. This system became known as feudalism.

In December 1085, William started a new campaign. He wanted to learn about every part of his kingdom and how it had changed since 1066. The reason he wanted to know about the land and wealth of the kingdom was so that he could impose taxes on it. This giant survey was completed in 1086 and was known as the Domesday Book. It gives a detailed picture of Norman England.

The Domesday Book was completed just a year before William died during yet another military expedition in France. By this time, the Norman rule was secure. But William's son, William Rufus, still made sure he was crowned quickly before anyone else could claim the throne.

## A LASTING IMPACT

William the Conqueror led the last successful invasion of England of the past 950 years. We can still see signs of the Norman Conquest today, and not just in the ruins of castles and monasteries. The Anglo-Saxons' language was called Old English but it was completely different from the English we speak now. The Normans brought the French language to England. Just as the Norman invaders married and mixed with the English, so did their language. Over the centuries, this mixture, along with words from later settlers in Britain, formed the modern British culture and language.

# THE DOMESDAY BOOK

The Domesday Book of 1086 tells us all about Norman England and how it changed after the Norman Conquest. We know that the king controlled 17 per cent of the land in England. The rest of the land was given to his barons, who paid rent to the king.

The 11 most powerful barons controlled a quarter of the land but their estates were spread around the country so that they did not become too powerful in any region. Almost all of the 1,400 main landholders in the Domesday Book came from Normandy.

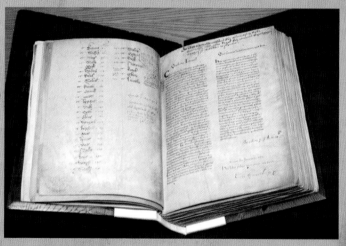

*The original Domesday Book is held in the National Archives.*

# INDEX

# GLOSSARY

**ANGLO-SAXONS** — invaders and settlers, including Angles, Saxons and Jutes, who came to Britain from northern Europe and ruled England before the Normans

**ARCHBISHOP** — senior figure in the Christian Church, with authority over other bishops

**CORONATION** — ceremony in which someone is formally crowned to become king or queen

**DESCENDANT** — relative from a later generation, such as a child or grandchild of someone

**EARL** — senior noble or chieftain who rules a territory on behalf of a king

**HAUBERK** — piece of chain-mail armour either covering only the neck and shoulders or as a full-length coat or tunic

**HEIR** — someone who will take over the responsibilities or titles of another person on their death, such as an heir to the throne who will take over as monarch from a previous king or queen

**HOSTAGE** — prisoner who will only be released if another condition is met, for example to make sure that an enemy does not go back on a deal

**HOUSECARL** — full-time soldier and member of the personal bodyguard of an Anglo-Saxon king

**KNIGHT** — someone who served his lord as a soldier on horseback

**MAIM** — wound or injure someone seriously, such as by cutting off one of their limbs

**MEDIEVAL** — adjective to describe something from the Middle Ages, which was the period of history from around 1000 to 1453 AD

**MONARCH** — king or queen

**MONASTERY** — building or community of buildings where monks who take religious vows live

**NOBLE** — member of leading or upper class within a society

**NORMAN** — people who live or lived in Normandy, which is now a region of northern France

**OATH** — sacred promise

**SIEGE** — blockade of a city in order to force the people living in there to surrender their control of it

**TAX** — money collected by a government from the people it governs

# TIMELINE

## 1016

King Cnut seizes crown of England after death of King Aethelred. Aethelred's younger sons Edward and Alfred escape to Normandy

## 1028

Birth of William, later Duke of Normandy and King of England

## 1035

William becomes Duke of Normandy after death of his father Duke Robert

## 1042

After deaths of King Cnut and his sons, Edward returns to England and is crowned king

## 1066

**5 Jan:** Death of King Edward the Confessor

**6 Jan:** Harold Godwinson is crowned as King Harold II of England

**Apr:** People in England and Normandy see a comet in the sky, which the English see as a bad omen

**25 Sep:** Harold's army defeats army of his brother Tostig and Harald Hardrada at Battle of Stamford Bridge

**27 Sep:** William's invasion fleet sets sail from Normandy

**14 Oct:** Norman army defeats Harold's forces in the Battle of Hastings

**25 Dec:** William is crowned King William I of England

## 1069

Series of rebellions in northern England against Norman rule

## 1070

Odo of Bayeux, half-brother of King William, orders Bayeux Tapestry to be created

## 1086

The Domesday Book, a full survey of England before and after the Norman Conquest, is finished

## 1087

William the Conqueror dies from a riding injury while on a military campaign in France

## 1047

Duke William defeats his Norman enemies at the Battle of Val-ès-Dunes

## 1051

King Edward banishes Earl Godwine and his family. According to William, Edward names him as heir to the throne of England

## 1053

Earl Godwine dies and his son Harold is the new Earl of Wessex

## 1064

Harold visits Normandy, possibly because he is shipwrecked, and swears to help William become the next King of England

# SELECT BIBLIOGRAPHY

*A History of Britain Volume 1: At the Edge of the World? 5000 BC – AD 1603*, Simon Schama (BBC Worldwide, 2000)

BBC History > The Normans
**www.bbc.co.uk/history/british/normans/**

*Conquest and Colonization: The Normans in Britain 1066–1100*, Brian Golding (Palgrave, 2001)

National Archives > World of Domesday
**www.nationalarchives.gov.uk/domesday/world-of-domesday**

*The Battle of Hastings*, Harriet Harvey Wood (Atlantic Books, 2008)

*The Norman Conquest*, Marc Morris (Hutchinson, 2012)

UK Battlefields Resource Centre > Battle of Hastings
**www.battlefieldstrust.com/resource-centre/viking/battleview.asp?BattleFieldId=17**

# WEBSITES

**www.bayeuxtapestry.org.uk**
Discover more about the Bayeux Tapestry, which tells the Norman side of the story of the Norman Conquest.

**www.bbc.co.uk/history/british/normans/launch_gms_battle_hastings.shtml**
Play this Battle of Hastings game from the BBC.

**www.nationalarchives.gov.uk/domesday/world-of-domesday**
Find out what England was like just after the Norman Conquest with this website from the National Archives.

# FURTHER READING

*Anglo-Saxons and Vikings* (Usborne History of Britain), Hazel Maskell and Abigail Wheatley (Usborne, 2012)

*Battle Books: Hastings*, Gary Smailes (Franklin Watts, 2011)

*Eyewitness: Arms and Armour* (Dorling Kindersley, 2011)

*Medieval Cathedral* (A Spectacular Visual Guide), Fiona MacDonald and John James (Book House, 2009)

*The History Detective Investigates the Normans and the Battle of Hastings,*

raintree 🍃

a Capstone company — publishers for children

CONTENT CONSULTANT:
Dr Linsey Hunter
Lecturer and Teaching Assistant at the University of the
Highlands and Islands

BY NICK HUNTER

# THE ANGLO-SAXON PERSPECTIVE

# NORMAN CONQUEST

## The Split History of the

A PERSPECTIVES FLIP BOOK

## ABOUT THE AUTHOR:

Nick Hunter grew up in East Anglia. He studied history at the University of St Andrews and spent many years as a publisher of children's non-fiction books before becoming a writer. He writes about history and many other subjects, enjoying the challenge and responsibility of inspiring young readers and explaining the world to them. Nick lives in Oxford with his wife and two sons.

## SOURCE NOTES:

**The Norman perspective**
Page 5, line 14 *(pp. 20–21)*; page 8, line 12 *(p.113)*; page 14, line 12 *(p.146)*; page 14, line 16 *(p.151)*; page 17, panel, line 10 *(p.47)*: *The Norman Conquest*, Marc Morris (Hutchinson, 2012)

Page 10, line 6 *(p.91)*; page 15, panel, line 5 *(p.93)*: *A History of Britain Volume 1: At the Edge of the World? 3000 BC–AD 1603*, Simon Schama (BBC Worldwide, 2000)

Page 17, panel, line 4: http://spartacus-educational.com/MEDhauberk.htm

Page 26, line 11: www.bbc.co.uk/history/british/normans/hudson_norman_01.shtml

**The Anglo-Saxon Perspective**
Page 11, line 3: Schama, page 89

Page 11, line 7: Morris, page 131

Page 28, line 3: www.bbc.co.uk/history/british/normans/after_01.shtml#seven

# Contents

# THE ENEMY WITHIN

*I*n 1066, England's army suffered one of the most disastrous defeats in its history. Invaders from Normandy, led by a duke with grand ideas about being a king, brought an end to the Anglo-Saxon era. The Anglo-Saxon royal family, which had ruled England for hundreds of years, was destroyed. The brutal kings of a foreign power – the Normans – replaced them.

Foreign raiders had been trying to conquer England long before 1066. King Alfred the Great had fought off Viking invaders from northern Europe at the Battle of Edington in 878 AD. Viking settlers still had their own land in the north-east of England, called the Danelaw, but Alfred's descendants had extended Anglo-Saxon rule across all of England.

In the early 11th century, the Vikings took revenge. They raided England's coast with bigger armies than ever before in efforts to rule the whole country. In 1016, Viking King Cnut became King of England. Cnut secured his position by murdering members of the Anglo-Saxon royal family.

Cnut also married Emma, the widow of the previous king, Aethelred, to strengthen his power. The only other survivors of the Anglo-Saxon royal family were Aethelred's two youngest sons. Aged no more than thirteen, they fled across the English Channel to Normandy when Cnut took power.

King Cnut was happy to give power to Viking and English barons, as long as they were loyal to him. The king had already shown that he could be ruthless with his enemies. Earl Godwine recognized the importance of staying on the right side of Cnut. He became one of Cnut's most powerful supporters.

## EDWARD AND EARL GODWINE

In 1042, after the death of Cnut and his sons, Aethelred's son Edward returned from Normandy to claim the throne. Edward had been abroad for more than 25 years. The new king realized that he would have to control Godwine and the other barons. The barons were suspicious of the many Norman friends that the new king brought with him.

*The personal seal of Godwine carried great authority.*

## ANGLO-SAXON ENGLAND

When Edward was crowned at Winchester in 1042, he became king of a country that was doing well. England's administration was well organized into districts called shires and counties. The king and his nobles used this organization to make laws, collect taxes and draft men for military service.

Trade and commerce flourished in the Anglo-Saxon kingdom. The Roman Catholic Church had a powerful position in society and most art was created to glorify God, including handwritten and beautifully illustrated books created by monks.

Compared to Anglo-Saxon England, Normandy was a brutal, violent place, where the dukes imposed power by force from behind the walls of their stone castles.

## GODWINE IN CHARGE

In Anglo-Saxon England, power and land went hand in hand. A powerful noble such as Earl Godwine did not just own the land, he controlled all the less powerful lords and peasants who lived there. Earl Godwine owned a lot of land and was used to getting his own way. By helping Edward to become king, Godwine hoped to wield even more power. He even arranged for Edward to marry his daughter Edith. Edward was not happy about it, but Godwine didn't give him much choice. He needed Godwine's support if he wanted to keep his throne.

In 1051, King Edward finally got his chance to cut Godwine down to size. The Anglo-Saxon earls were fed up with Edward's

Norman friends. When one of them, Eustace of Boulogne, was attacked in the port of Dover, Godwine was ordered to punish the people of the town. He refused and Edward banished the Godwine family abroad.

Godwine's disgrace did not last long. Other earls supported him and wanted him to return. In September 1052, the disgraced earl sailed up the River Thames into London. Edward could not find anyone prepared to stop Godwine. The earl was back in charge and Edward's Norman friends were forced to leave the country and give up all their lands.

*Saxon craftsmen created intricate jewellery and weapons, such as these items from the Staffordshire Hoard discovered in 2009.*

While Edward was still king in theory, Godwine held power after his triumphant return. But, just a year later, Earl Godwine was dead. The *Anglo-Saxon Chronicle* says that Godwine collapsed while he was having dinner with the king and died soon afterwards. But Godwine's sons were not about to let go of his power.

## THE NEXT GENERATION

Godwine's eldest surviving son, Harold, became Earl of Wessex. This meant that he controlled most of southern England. Harold soon installed his brother Tostig as earl in the important northern region of Northumbria. Harold also found powerful positions for his other brothers. Their sister was married to the king. With his family taking most of the top jobs, Harold was unchallenged as the most powerful man in England.

While Harold was building his power base, King Edward gave up trying to control him. Edward is now known as Edward the Confessor because he devoted the later years of his rule to the Church. Edward is often shown on his knees praying. In fact, the Church was one place where the Godwines could not gain control.

## TROUBLE WITH TOSTIG

In 1065, Harold Godwinson's power and family loyalty was put to the test. His brother Tostig had made himself very unpopular as the Earl of Northumbria. Tostig had raided monasteries and raised unfair taxes to pay for his own private army. But this army had not done much to protect the people from raids over the border from Scotland.

*Edward's greatest project was to build a splendid cathedral to the west of London, called West Minster. Westminster Abbey is still standing today.*

Eventually, the Northumbrians had had enough and rebelled against Tostig. Would Harold back him or would he support the rebels, allied with the powerful Earl of Mercia? Harold decided the rebels were a better choice and Tostig was forced into exile, vowing revenge on his brother.

Harold may have been thinking that he needed support from the Earl of Mercia for his political career. King Edward was getting old and Harold had his eye on the top job – he wanted to be king.

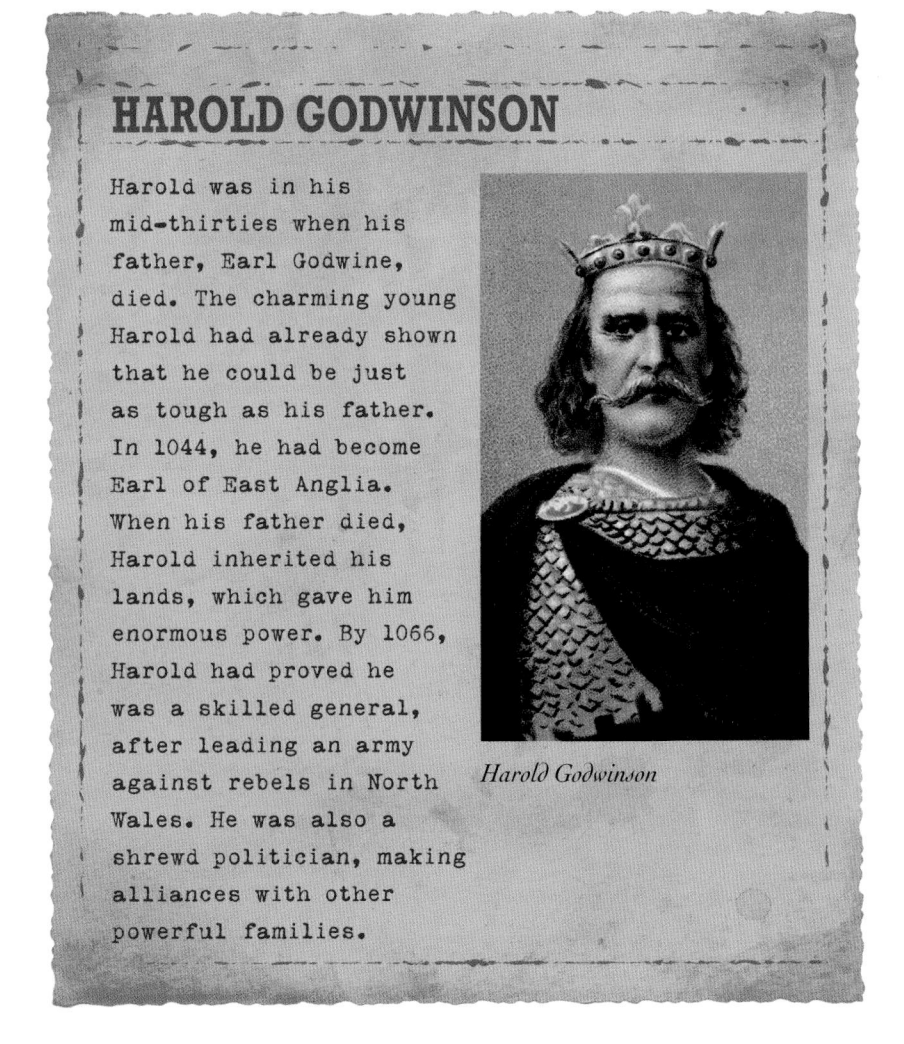

## HAROLD GODWINSON

Harold was in his mid-thirties when his father, Earl Godwine, died. The charming young Harold had already shown that he could be just as tough as his father. In 1044, he had become Earl of East Anglia. When his father died, Harold inherited his lands, which gave him enormous power. By 1066, Harold had proved he was a skilled general, after leading an army against rebels in North Wales. He was also a shrewd politician, making alliances with other powerful families.

*Harold Godwinson*

# CLAIMS TO THE THRONE

By the end of 1065, King Edward was dying. In his final days, Edward issued a warning. He had been visited by two monks in a dream, who warned him that evil spirits would rule England for a year and a day . Visions and omens like this were taken very seriously in the 11th century. England's ruling families were right to be worried about the future, because no one knew who would be the next king.

## CHOOSING A KING

The old king had no children to inherit the throne when he died. Since the time of King Cnut, the crowning of a new monarch had been a complicated process, often resulting in violence. The new king should be someone with a family link to the old king, preferably chosen by him. The leading nobles also had to approve the choice; without their support no king could survive for long.

Harold Godwinson was just one of several powerful men who claimed the throne when Edward died on 5 January 1066. Edgar Atheling was the old king's great nephew. He was descended from the kings of Wessex, just as Edward the Confessor was. However, Edgar was living in Europe and had no army or powerful friends to help him take the throne.

# HAROLD IN NORMANDY

Two of the candidates for the English crown had already met. In 1064, Harold Godwinson journeyed to Normandy. No one can be sure why he went there, and a storm may have forced him to land. Another theory is that he planned to win the freedom of two supporters who were imprisoned in Normandy. Godwinson was captured and taken to Duke William of Normandy.

William believed that he should be the next king of England, but his claim was weak. William had a distant link to Edward's family, but other possible kings were much closer. He was unlikely to get the support of England's earls, who had already done all they could to get rid of Edward's Norman advisers. William's best hope was his claim that Edward had promised him the throne in 1051, around the time that the Godwine family had been banished from England.

In 1064, Harold had to keep the peace with William to ensure he would return to England alive. Most of what we know about Harold's time in Normandy was written or pictured by Normans. The Bayeux Tapestry is an enormous embroidered piece of cloth. Its embroidered scenes depict the events leading up to the Norman conquest. It tells the Normans' version of their invasion of England. One scene shows that Harold helped the Normans in a military campaign in Brittany, west of Normandy.

# DEAL OR NO DEAL?

The Bayeux Tapestry also shows Harold swearing an oath. This was not unusual for a noble in a foreign land. Harold was agreeing to be loyal to William while he was in Normandy. But according to the Anglo-Saxons, Harold was not agreeing to help William become King of England. Harold wanted to be king himself, so why would he agree to help William? The Tapestry shows Harold swearing his oath on holy relics, which would make the oath a solemn promise, but we can't be sure if that really happened.

*Harold fought with William on a military expedition to Brittany. There, he is supposed to have rescued some of William's soldiers from quicksand around Mont St Michel. This is shown here in the Bayeux Tapestry.*

William was not the only a foreigner who wanted to be king of England. Harald Hardrada was one of the most feared warriors in Europe. He believed he had a strong claim to the throne going back to the time of King Cnut. Cnut was said to have promised the throne of England to the kings of Norway, and Hardrada was always up for a fight.

## HAROLD'S CLAIM

Harold Godwinson was the most powerful man in England. He believed his claim to the throne was better than anyone else's. His sister had been married to Edward the Confessor. Harold claimed that Edward had chosen him to be the next king, and English chronicles support his claim. He had also worked very hard to make sure he had the support of the other earls, even if it meant upsetting his brother Tostig. To seal the deal, Harold married Ealdgyth, sister of the earls of Northumbria and Mercia.

*The Witenagemot advised the king and had an important role in choosing any new king.*

# DEFENDING ENGLAND

*H*arold decided that the best way to clear up the debate about who should be the next king was to act quickly. On 6 January 1066, he was crowned King Harold II of England. It was a busy time at Westminster Abbey as the old king's funeral happened on the same day.

Coronations were not usually arranged so quickly, but Harold had good reason to hurry. Most people at the time believed that kings were chosen by God. Once Harold was crowned, anyone who tried to defeat him could be accused of breaking God's law. King Harold knew that there were plenty of rivals out to get him, and England needed a strong leader.

Soon after his coronation, Harold travelled north to York, probably to deal with people who were unhappy about his seizing power. Harold could deal with opposition in England, but he knew that the greatest threat came from abroad, from Norway and Normandy. By taking the crown, Harold had made some powerful enemies.

# SURPRISE ATTACK

William, Duke of Normandy sent a message to remind Harold that he, William, had been promised the English crown. Harold did not bother to reply. Soon after his coronation, Harold's spies in Normandy informed him that Duke William was building a fleet of ships. This could mean only one thing – invasion.

However, the first fleet to attack southern England in 1066 was not led by William but by Harold's younger brother Tostig. Tostig's forces probably sailed from Flanders, in modern Belgium, where he had been living. They raided towns along the south and east coasts, but Tostig had little support in England. He would need a powerful ally to help him get his revenge.

Harold was an experienced general before he became king and he wasted no time assembling the forces to defend his kingdom. He stationed soldiers and ships along the south coast to repel invaders from the south. He also set about recruiting a large army from across the country. In Anglo-Saxon England, the lords who controlled different parts of the country provided men from their lands to serve the king. Along with his 3,000 elite troops, Harold could call on thousands of part-time warriors. This army was called the Fyrd.

# THE WAITING GAME

Harold would be ready for William whenever he attacked. In April, the English saw a comet in the sky (now known as Halley's Comet). All agreed that this strange moving star was a bad omen, but there was no sign of the Normans. Through the summer of 1066, the English waited.

*Almost everyone in Anglo-Saxon society had to help with the harvest.*

Most of Harold's part-time soldiers were also farmers. If they were waiting for Norman invaders, how could they collect the harvest? If the crops were left to rot in the fields, people would starve. The longer they waited, the more restless they became. On 8 September, Harold allowed his soldiers to return home.

It was bad timing. Just a few days later, Harold received news of a new threat. Harald Hardrada, the "Thunderbolt of the North", had landed in Northumbria with 10,000 men. Harold's troublesome brother Tostig was supporting Hardrada. Harold would have to face the fearsome Norwegian in the north, but he would be leaving the south coast undefended.

# STAMFORD BRIDGE

Harold summoned his part-time soldiers as he hurried north. His elite troops, or housecarls, were always ready, but his other troops might not be prepared in time.

On 20 September, Eadwin and Morcar, the Earls of Mercia and Northumbria, were defeated at Fulford near York. Although both of the earls escaped with their lives, unlike many of their men, only Harold could stop the invaders now.

Harald Hardrada decided not to destroy the city of York, but he demanded that its people should provide hostages to stop them rebelling against the invaders. The hostages had to be sent to a nearby place called Stamford Bridge. When Hardrada arrived to meet them, he got a shock. They were not met by a few hostages but by King Harold's huge army.

Harold had assembled his army and marched north in less than a week. Although Hardrada had won the previous battle, he and his forces had had little time to recover. They may not even have been wearing their full armour. Harold's army won a crushing victory. Both Harald Hardrada and Tostig were killed. Hundreds of ships had carried the invaders from Norway, but just 24 were needed to take the survivors home. The battle was the last defeat for the Vikings on English soil.

There was no time to celebrate. As his exhausted men recovered from the struggle at Stamford Bridge, Harold received more bad news. The wind had changed in the English Channel, meaning that the Norman fleet could set sail to start their attack on England. William was on his way.

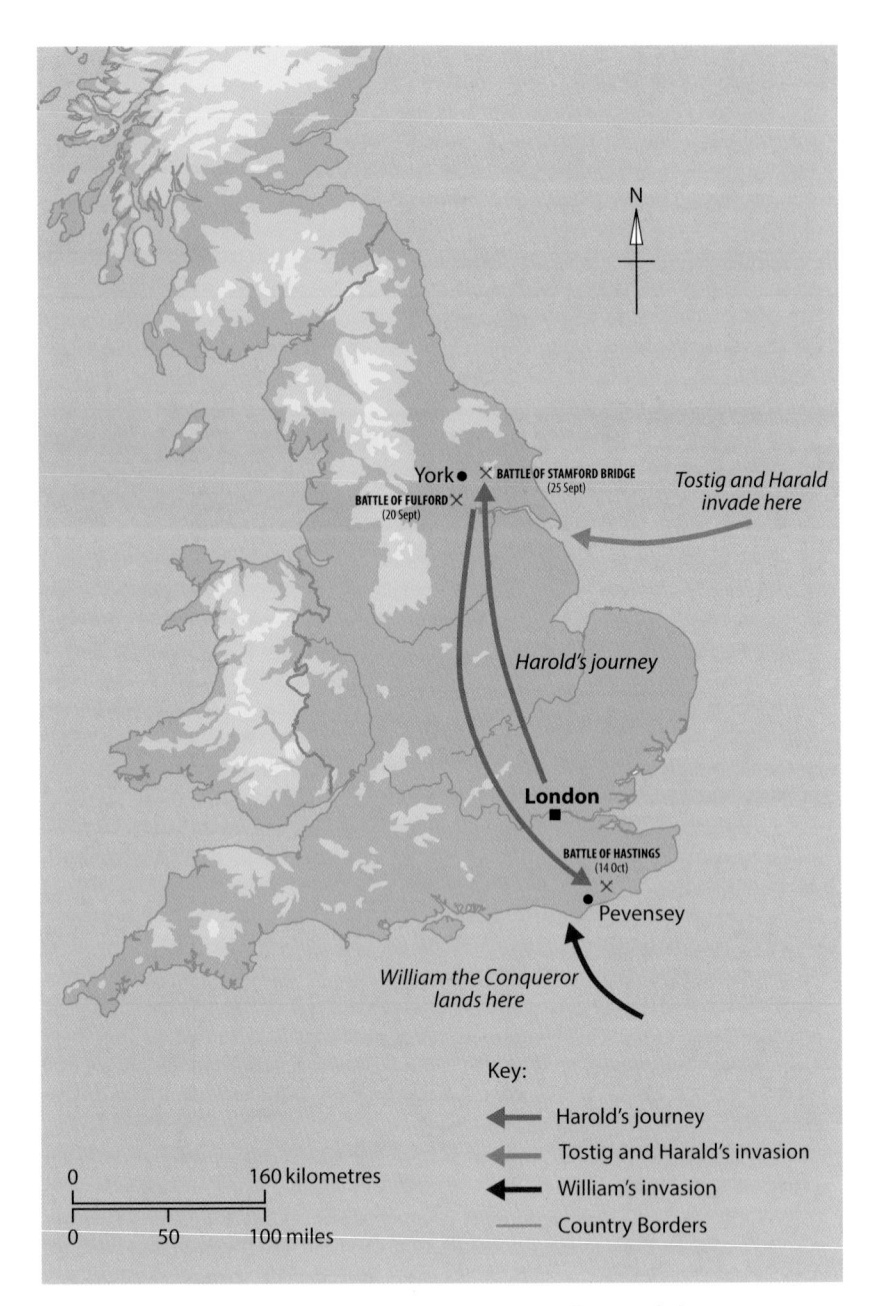

York•  ✕ BATTLE OF STAMFORD BRIDGE
            (25 Sept)

BATTLE OF FULFORD ✕
(20 Sept)

*Tostig and Harald
invade here*

*Harold's journey*

**London** ■

BATTLE OF HASTINGS
(14 Oct)
✕
• Pevensey

*William the Conqueror
lands here*

Key:

⬅ Harold's journey
⬅ Tostig and Harald's invasion
⬅ William's invasion
— Country Borders

0           160 kilometres

0     50     100 miles

*This map shows Harold, William and Tostig and Harald's travels during 1066.
Harold and his army had to cover long distances on foot or horseback to face their
two enemies.*

# DEFEAT AT HASTINGS

When he heard of the Norman invasion, Harold and his army were near York, around 435 kilometres (270 miles) from the south coast where the Norman attack was expected. The king's journey south had to be just as quick as his marathon march north to the Battle of Stamford Bridge.

The Normans landed on 28 September, but Harold did not receive the news for several days. As he rushed south, Harold heard stories of the destruction the invaders were causing as they attacked towns in search of food and anything else they could get their hands on. Harold could not allow this to continue. He would have to meet the Normans in battle.

On the morning of 14 October 1066, King Harold faced the invaders across a battlefield just north of Hastings. The site was later named Battle. Harold had been planning to surprise the Normans and attack their camp at Hastings. William had heard about the plan and surprised the English by marching his army north to meet Harold's army.

# BATTLE TACTICS

Harold's army was organized in three wedges on the high ground of Senlac Ridge. The English soldiers were exhausted after their long march. The Norman army may also have outnumbered them, although no one can be sure. The English army's best chance of winning was to form a wall of shields to defend themselves from the Norman attacks. This tactic had been successful before.

*Harold's soldiers defended themselves with broad wooden shields. They fought with spears, swords and skull-cracking battle-axes.*

## WHY DID HAROLD FIGHT?

Harold did not have to meet his enemy at the Battle of Hastings. He had just fought off one attempted invasion in the north. His troops needed time to recover. If he had waited a few weeks, Harold could have called on a much larger army that would have overwhelmed William's invading force. Instead, Harold decided to face William before he could fight his way deep into England. Maybe he believed that his English warriors would be too powerful for the Normans.

King Harold fought at the centre of his army, where his troops could see him. The housecarls stood firm in the front line, armed with spears and heavy two-handed axes. They had not faced knights on horseback before, but they believed that the shield wall would stand firm.

If the Normans could not break the wall of shields, they would stay trapped on the south coast of England, and would run out of food and supplies. The high ground gave Harold's army a huge advantage when facing a cavalry charge.

## CLOSE TO VICTORY

For attack after attack, the Norman foot soldiers and cavalry could not break through the English defences. After a few hours, the attackers were exhausted and began to lose hope. Rumours spread around the battlefield that Duke William had been killed. One section of the Norman army started to fall back, pursued by many of the English defenders who could now sense victory.

Just at the moment when victory seemed to be in their grasp, the English were in great danger. By following those Normans who had started to retreat, the previously unbreakable shield wall was broken. Harold had counted on defence to win the day. Instead, William rallied his troops and they fought back ferociously.

The battle raged all day. After their previous retreat had broken the English line, the Normans fell back again, before turning on the English warriors who followed them. The wall of shields was gradually weakened.

The decisive moment came when King Harold was killed. The Bayeux Tapestry shows an arrow hitting him in the eye. Some accounts of the battle argue that Harold was killed deliberately, before he could leave the battle and fight another day.

The king's two brothers were also killed. Without their leaders, defeat was inevitable. The part-time soldiers of the Fyrd fled as fast as possible to save their own lives and return to their families.

*We can't be sure if Harold was killed by an arrow hitting his eye, but it is a theme that has been shown in many illustrations over the centuries. Harold's death sealed the defeat of his army.*

# A BLOODY END

The brutal Norman knights followed the English as they fled, spilling as much blood as they could. The exhausted English soldiers were no match for the Norman pursuers on horseback. As the English lay dead and dying, Normans scoured the battlefield for valuable weapons and armour. They then set out on a reign of terror across the country. The Normans would be happy with nothing less than the destruction of Anglo-Saxon England.

Those English soldiers who were lucky enough to escape from the battlefield returned home with terrible stories of what they had seen. After the Normans' crushing victory, no one would be able to stop them. But what about the northern earls and their army, who had helped to defeat Harald Hardrada?

*This section of the Bayeux Tapestry shows a mother and child fleeing as their home is burned by the Normans.*

# THE END OF ANGLO-SAXON ENGLAND

King Harold and the Godwines may not have survived the Battle of Hastings but the powerful earls in the north, who had not fought at Hastings, were ready to take up the fight against the invaders. They had their own candidate for the crown in Edgar Atheling. The Norman army was weaker after their losses in the battle.

William still had to seal control of the main settlements in southern England. His troops marched to Dover and Canterbury in Kent. Many towns submitted to William without a fight. They could not defend themselves and knew that they would be destroyed if they tried to resist. English sources such as the *Anglo-Saxon Chronicle* state that the Normans left a trail of destruction across southern England.

London was different. There was only one bridge into the city across the River Thames in the city and many of its English warriors were committed to fighting off the foreign king. Their resolve weakened as they saw the damage the Normans unleashed across England. By December 1066, the most powerful earls and archbishops in the country surrendered to William without a fight. They were more interested in saving their own lives and privileges than they were in fighting the invaders.

# THE NEW KING

The Duke of Normandy was crowned King William I at Westminster Abbey on Christmas Day 1066. The Anglo-Saxon kingdom of England lay in ruins, but some people were unwilling to give in to Norman rule.

After 1066, the nobles who had helped William to victory at the Battle of Hastings were given huge estates across England. William's Norman knights tried to impose their will on the English, taking land and building hundreds of stone castles.

On the Welsh border, Eadric the Wild was not about to hand over his lands without a fight. King Harold's sons also launched attacks on the west coast from their base in Ireland. King Sweyn II of Denmark thought he had just as good a claim to the throne as King William. He launched an unsuccessful invasion with 200 ships landing in Northumbria.

In Northumbria, many northerners felt closer to the Vikings than the English, especially as many of their ancestors were Vikings. London seemed a very long way away, and Normandy was even further. They certainly did not want to be bowing and speaking French to a king who had not defeated them.

In 1069, Northumbrian rebels, with the support of the kings of Scotland and Denmark, murdered the Norman troops stationed in Durham before marching to York. Earls Edwin and Morcar, who had surrendered to William but now decided to fight, soon joined the northern rebels. Followers of the rebel Hereward the Wake carried off treasures from the cathedral in Peterborough.

# HEREWARD THE WAKE

One of the most famous Anglo-Saxon rebels may
not have existed at all. Normans took Hereward
the Wake's family lands after 1066. Hereward is
believed to have attacked the Normans from his
base on the Isle of Ely - an island in the middle
of marshes in the east of England. He became a
symbol of resistance to Norman power, similar
to the later legend of Robin Hood. However, the
events of his life were written down many years
after his death so we can't be sure whether they
are true.

*Hereward the Wake*

# WILLIAM'S REVENGE

William reacted savagely to the northern sieges. He attacked York with an overwhelming force and "ravaged the city", according to an English source. The people of Northumbria faced the worst revenge of all, even though most ordinary people had done nothing to support the rebellion. The Normans destroyed towns and burned crops. Without food or homes, the people were left to die of starvation.

Finally, in 1072, Scotland faced its own brief Norman invasion. Edgar Atheling, who had been a possible king of England in 1066, was sheltering with Scottish King Malcolm III. William's attack forced Malcolm to give up this last pocket of resistance and accept William as King of England.

## ORDERIC VITALIS

Much of our knowledge of the Norman invasion is based on accounts that were written down in the years after 1066, and the wonderful images of the Bayeux Tapestry. All of these written sources were created once William was king. Very few people could write at the time so when history was written down, it was almost always by monks. A monk would have to be very brave, or foolish, to write the story from the Anglo-Saxon point of view after William's victory. The closest thing we have to an Anglo-Saxon view written at the time is the work of Orderic Vitalis, a monk with a Norman father and English mother. His account is one of the few to criticize the Norman invaders' violence.

*While the Normans brutally defeated any rebels, not much changed for ordinary people. Villagers might pay their taxes to a new lord but the daily struggle to grow food and stay alive was unaltered.*

After 1072, the English largely accepted their new rulers. The monks and others who told the story of Anglo-Saxon England's defeat did everything they could to promote William and his Norman followers as the rightful rulers of England. The bloody events of 1066 and the years that followed could not change the fact that most of the people were still English. They were the descendants of Anglo-Saxon settlers who simply had a new lord who replaced customs and the language, Old English, with new customs and a new language: French.

# INDEX